Please return/renew this item by the
last date shown to avoid a charge.
Books may also be renewed by phone
and Internet. May not be renewed if
required by another reader.

BARNET
LONDON BOROUGH
www.libraries.barnet.gov.uk

K124

Simple Maths

Subtracting and Taking Away

Richard Leffingwell

www.raintreepublishers.co.uk

Visit our website to find out more information about **Raintree** books.

To order:
- ☎ Phone 44 (0) 1865 888112
- 🖹 Send a fax to 44 (0) 1865 314091
- 🖥 Visit the Raintree Bookshop at **www.raintreepublishers.co.uk** to browse our catalogue and order online.

First published in Great Britain by Raintree, Halley Court, Jordan Hill, Oxford OX2 8EJ, part of Harcourt Education.
Raintree is a registered trademark of Harcourt Education Ltd.

Editorial: Diyan Leake and Cassie Mayer
Design: Joanna Hinton-Malivoire and The Partnership
Picture Research: Erica Newbery
Production: Duncan Gilbert

Originated by Modern Age
Printed and bound in China by South China Printing Company

10 digit ISBN 1 4062 0391 2
13 digit ISBN 978 4062 0391 2

10 09 08 07 06
10 9 8 7 6 5 4 3 2 1

British Library Cataloguing in Publication Data
Leffingwell, Richard
Subtracting and Taking Away
513.2'12
A full catalogue record for this book is available from the British Library.

Acknowledgements

The publishers would like to thank the following for permission to reproduce photographs: Alamy pp. **14**, **15**, **16**; Getty Images (Photodisc Red/ Davies & Starr) pp. **5**, **6**, **7**, **8**; Harcourt Education Ltd (www.mmstudios.co.uk) pp. **4**, **9–12**, **17–22**, back cover

Cover photographs reproduced with permission of Photolibrary (Brand X/Burke Triolo) and Jupiter Images (FoodPix).

The publishers would like to thank Patti Barber, Specialist in Early Childhood and Primary Education, Institute of Education, University of London, for her assistance in the preparation of this book.

Every effort has been made to contact copyright holders of any material reproduced in this book. Any omissions will be rectified in subsequent printings if notice is given to the publishers.

The paper used to print this book comes from sustainable resources.

Contents

What is subtracting?

Subtracting can help you find out how many things you have left.

Subtracting is useful in many ways.

Subtracting shells

Pretend that you have 5 shells.

You take 2 shells and give them to a friend.

$$5 - 2 = ?$$

How many shells do you have now?

Take away 2 shells from the group of 5.

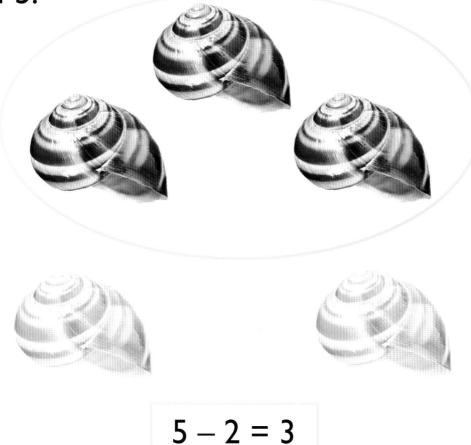

$$5 - 2 = 3$$

Now count to see how many you have left.

There are 3 left.

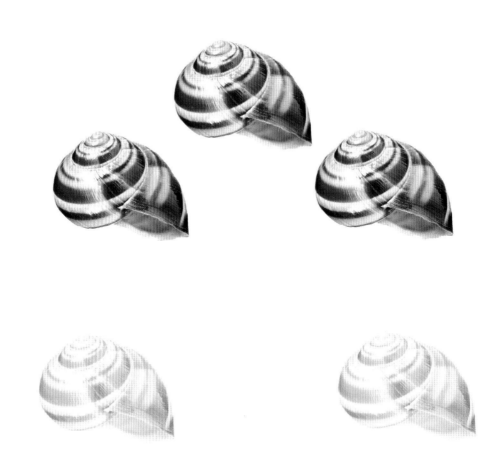

When you take away items from a group, you are subtracting them.

Subtracting stones

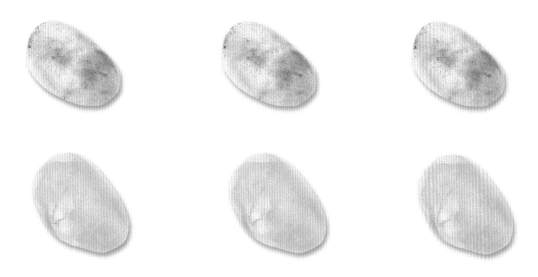

$$6 - 2 = ?$$

Pretend that you have 6 stones and give 2 of them away.

How can you find out how many are left?

You can draw a picture and count the stones.

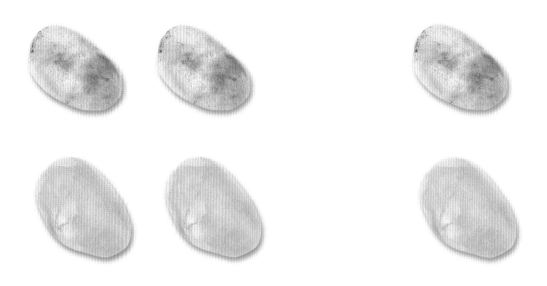

$$6 - 2 = 4$$

You have 4 left.

How else can you find out how many are left?

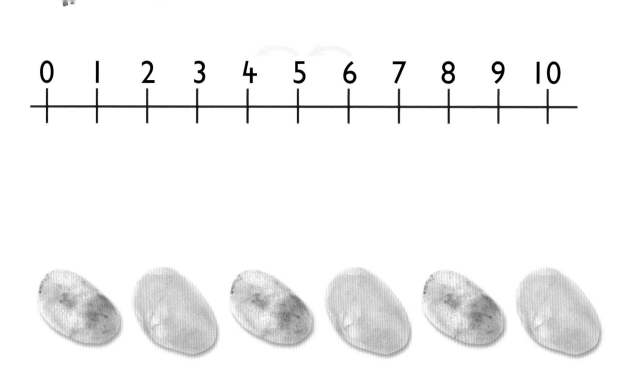

You can count back.

Count back once for each stone that was taken away.

Start counting back from 6.

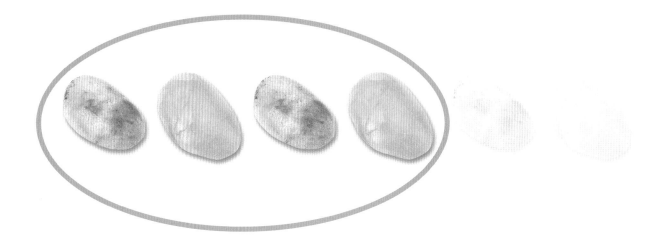

$$6 - 2 = 4$$

You took away 2 stones.

You have 4 stones left.

1   2   3   4   5   6

$$6 - 2 = 4$$

Counting back is when you count backwards from the number you started with.

You count back once for each thing that is taken away.

Subtracting leaves

Pretend that you have 4 leaves and give 1 away.

Find out how many leaves you have by counting back.

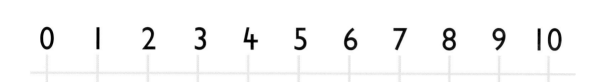

You started with 4 leaves.

Count back from 4.

Count back 1 time.

Count back for each leaf that is taken away.

You counted back 1 time.

You have 3 leaves left.

Comparing groups

Pretend that you have 5 pencils.

Your friend has 3 pencils.

How many more pencils do you have?

To solve the problem, compare the two groups.

When you compare two groups, you are subtracting.

Look at the two groups.

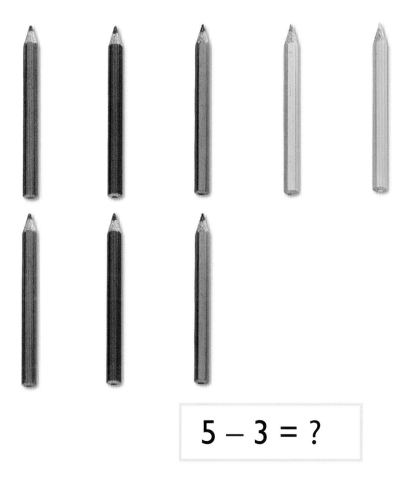

5 − 3 = ?

Can you see how many more pencils there are in your group?

You can see that 5 is 2 more than 3.

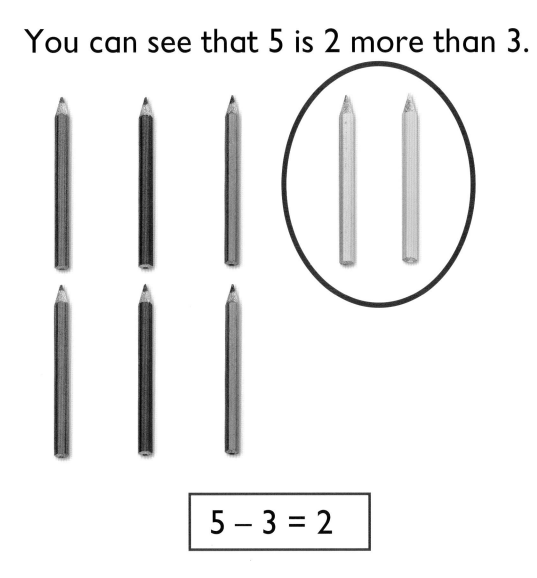

$$5 - 3 = 2$$

You have 2 more pencils.

Subtraction helps you find out how many of something is left.

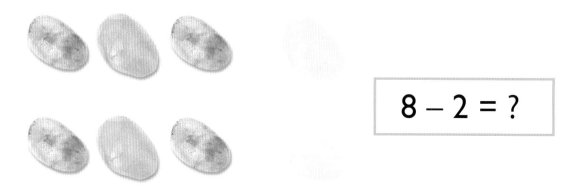

$$8 - 2 = ?$$

You also subtract when you compare two groups.

That way you find out how many more there are in the bigger group.

$$3 - 1 = ?$$

Quiz

Can you work out how many more red pencils there are?

Hint: Use the number line to count back.

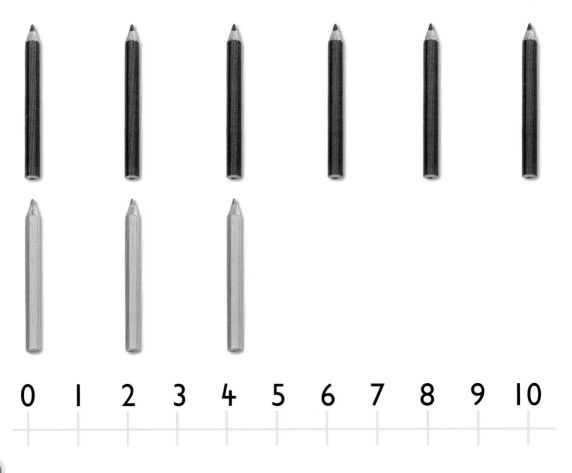

0 1 2 3 4 5 6 7 8 9 10

The minus sign

| − | You use this sign to show that you are taking one number away from another. |

$$3 - 2$$

When you take 2 away from 3, you get 1.

| = | You use the equals sign to show what 3 minus 2 is equal to. |

$$3 - 2 = 1$$

Index

Answer to the quiz on page 22
There are 3 more red pencils.

Note to parents and teachers

Reading non-fiction texts for information is an important part of a child's literacy development. Readers can be encouraged to ask simple questions and then use the text to find the answers. Most chapters in this book begin with a question. Read the questions together. Look at the pictures. Talk about what the answer might be. Then read the text to find out if your predictions were correct. To develop readers' enquiry skills, encourage them to think of other questions they might ask about the topic. Discuss where you could find the answers. Assist children in using the contents page, picture glossary and index to practise research skills and new vocabulary.

Titles in the **Simple Maths** series include.

Hardback 1 4062 0390 4
978 1 4062 0390 5

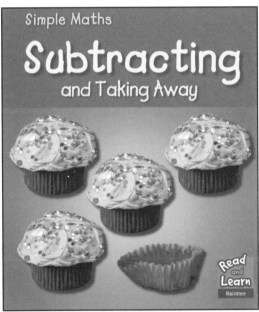

Hardback 1 4062 0391 2
978 1 4062 0391 2

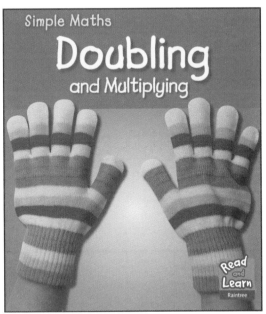

Hardback 1 4062 0392 0
978 1 4062 0392 9

Hardback 1 4062 0393 9
978 1 4062 0393 6

Find out more about the other titles in this series on our website www.raintreepublishers.co.uk